TO ALL THE CURIOUS ADVENTURERS

Hi there! My name is Joaquin (pronounced Wah-Keen) The Dog. My mom and dad named me Joaquin because they thought it was funny and sounds like "walking the dog". We all love to go for walks, and I love new adventures.

Recently I visited Boston, Massachusetts in the northeast USA where my mom grew up. Boston has so much history, good food, and water views. It was pretty cold, but I have my permanent fur coat to keep me warm while exploring.

There are so many old buildings in Boston. I went to Fanueil Hall and Quincy Market where there are lots of shops and places for snacks. It smelled so yummy! Fanueil Hall used to be a popular place where all the city people came to meet.

Back in the 1700s people in Boston threw tea off a big ship and into the water to protest being treated badly! It is now called the Boston Tea Party, and you can visit the museum and pretend to throw tea overboard. I also saw the biggest milk bottle EVER! They didn't have any puppy ice cream, though...

Paul Revere is famous for riding his horse to tell the soldiers "The British are coming!" during the Revolutionary War. Look at me in front of his statue! I tried to look just like the horse. What do you think? Did I do a good job?

Because Boston is so full of history and cool places, you can walk the Freedom Trail by following the red line and learning all about the city. I walked the Freedom Trail past the Old North Church, where Paul Revere used lanterns to tell soldiers how the British were arriving in Boston before the Battles of Lexington and Concord. The lanterns, "one if by land, two if by sea" helped the soldiers prepare and beat the British!

Boston has lots of Italian immigrants, and there's a whole neighborhood with Italian food and sweets called the North End. Here I am in front of the famous Mike's Pastry, known for its huge cannoli! Some people swear they're the best in the city, but others say Modern Pastry is the best. Next time I'm in Boston, I'll have to try both to see for myself.

Can you believe that building is over 300 years old?! That's the old state house, and it's one of the oldest public buildings in the whole country. Lots of politics took place in there, and now, lots of pictures take place outside of it. Say CHEESE!

The Boston Common is a gigantic park and the first public park in the US. I was so interested in all the squirrels. I couldn't stop staring (and chasing) them! The new state house is behind me and it has a shiny gold roof.

In the middle of the Boston Common is "The Frog Pond". In the winter, it becomes an ice skating rink!

That big blue building behind me tells Bostonians the daily weather by changing the colored lights. Solid blue means clear; flashing blue means cloudy; solid red means rain; and flashing red means snow!

Right next to the Boston Common is the Boston Public Garden. They have pretty plants and flowers. You can ride on a swan boat during the summer time. I visited the "Make Way for Ducklings" and pretended I was one of the baby ducklings! I also got to see the brick homes in Beacon Hill.

If you want a fun and unique way to see the city, you can take a Boston Duck Tour! You first drive through the city, then the bus goes into the water and turns into a boat!

A trip to Boston wouldn't be complete without a visit to Fenway Park, where the Boston Red Sox play catch. I also love to play catch! I kept hearing people say "play ball", and I was so excited. Fenway is the oldest original baseball stadium still in use!

Mom said maybe one day if I study really hard, I can go to Harvard. But the Bostonians said I need to be "wicked smaht" to go to Harvard, and that my cuteness would only get me so far...

I also visited some very important restaurants in Boston, Union Oyster House which is the oldest restaurant in Boston, the Omni Parker House where Boston Creme Pie was invented and Dunkin' Donuts, Boston's favorite eatery. I had the best time ever visiting Boston!

DID YOU KNOW?

Boston built the US' first subway system

The first Thanksgiving was celebrated in Boston in 1621

The first public beach and first US lighthouse were in Boston

Boston is home to over 40 colleges and universities

DID YOU KNOW?

The nickname “Bean Town” is from the city’s earliest settlers loving baked beans cooked in molasses

The first chocolate factory in the US was in Boston

Candle-pin bowling was invented in Boston

You can drive 90 ft underground in Boston in the Ted Williams Tunnel, the deepest in America

THE MASSACHUSETT TRIBE

WOMEN IN THE MASSACHUSETT TRIBE LIFE HAD A LOT OF RESPONSIBILITIES. THEY HUNTED, TRAPPED AND GATHERED FOOD AND MEDICINE. THE WOMEN TOOK CARE OF THE FIELDS AND TENDED THE HARVESTS AND CHILDREN HELPED KEEP THE BIRDS AWAY FROM THE PLANTED FIELDS. THE TRIBE LIVED IN WETUS (SUMMER HUTS) AND WINTER LONG HOUSES BUILT BY WOMEN. THE WOMEN ALSO MADE POTTERY, BASKETS, GATHERED WOOD, TENDED FIRES AND WERE IMPORTANT IN DECISION MAKING ALONG WITH THE MEN AND ELDERS WITHIN THE TRIBE.

THE MEN MINED, WHALED, FISHED, HUNTED AND PROTECTED THE TRIBE AND ITS TERRITORY.

THE MASSACHUSETT QUARRIES PROVIDED STONE, QUARTZ AND OTHER MINERALS FOR TOOLS, WEAPONS, AND OTHER ITEMS. QUARRY STONE, STONE TOOLS AND WEAPONS WERE ALSO USED IN TRADING.

WWW.MASACHUSETTTRIBE.ORG

LET'S BE FRIENDS!

WWW.JOAQUINTHEDOG.ORG

@JOAQUIN_AROUND_THE_WORLD

CPSIA information can be obtained
at www.ICGtesting.com
Printed in the USA
LVHW070446180422
716461LV00002B/21